pocket
cornwall

C000298822

Wild Food Foraging
in Cornwall and the Isles of Scilly

Rachel Lambert

Alison Hodge

Tor Mark

Alison Hodge is an imprint of Tor Mark,
United Downs Industrial Estate,
St Day, Redruth, Cornwall TR16 5HY

First published in 2015 by Alison Hodge
Reprinted 2015, 2017
This reprint 2019

ISBN 978 0 906720 96 7

Printed and bound in Great Britain
by Cambrian Printers

Title page: Harvested sea lettuce

Reverse front cover: Sea spinach

Reverse back cover: Foraging gorse flowers
Blackthorn plant
Wild fennel
Three-cornered leek

 Printed on FSC Mix

Acknowledgements

Many people have helped with bringing this book together, from recipe ideas to text reading, to general support of the idea, and tastings. In particular, I'd like to thank the following: Input into sustainability guidelines: Jon Brookes and Justin Whitehouse (National Trust), Jeremy Clitherow (Natural England Cornwall and Isles of Scilly). Recipe ideas and adaptations: Glenn Gatland (Head Chef, Tresco Estates) – Scilly Wild Spring Salad, Sharon Hogan and Darina Allen (Ballymaloe Cookery School) – adaptation of beef stew; Sara Readman-Smyth (Cotna Eco-Retreat) – Alexanders Risotto, Sorrel Dressing and Sloe Liqueur Chocolates; Euan Rodger (Tanglewood Kitchen) – Cod with Crispy Wild Leaves; Celt Net – adaptation of Cornish Nettle Soup. Editing text and reading the original book proposal: Ina Hartung, Stephanie Hirtenstein, Cat Jay, Sara Readman-Smyth and Terrie Sawyer.

All cultivated foods originate from wild food, though wild food can be stronger in flavour, some people may have reactions to certain plants. Brief medicinal uses are given for plants mentioned, please read and adhere to this and seek medical advice before using. In particular, avoid wild carrot seeds if pregnant, avoid sorrel if you have a tendency towards kidney stones, avoid alexanders if you have an allergy to celery and black mustard if you have an allergy to mustard.

Contents

Introduction

Foraging in Cornwall and the Isles of Scilly (IOS) has its own distinct flavour that I am unable to reproduce anywhere else in the UK or Europe – a distinctness I think worth celebrating, describing and guiding you through. Cornwall and the IOS are profoundly and proudly shaped by their immense coastline; the underlying granite, warm, humid climate, and strong winds. The plant life that has evolved here thrives in these environments. For me, walking, food, plants and the landscape provide a rich insight into an area; an intimate experience of the present, past and future. I hope that this book will help you not only to discover new tastes, but also to open your eyes to appreciating a Cornish or Scilly beach or hedgerow in a whole new way. Foraging is such a personal experience – the smells, tastes and textures interpreted by each individual's body with sometimes vastly differing results! One person's moment of taste heaven can truly unimpress another. However, during the years that I have taught foraging, I have built up a selection of plants and seaweeds that tend to be well received

– flavours that are savoured for their 'wow' effect; perhaps plants that people have heard of; scents that are reminiscent of something familiar; tastes that are refreshing, subtle, or just downright moreish. I have been influenced by plants that can be found in abundance: ones that you can expect to see in the natural, predominantly coastal areas of Cornwall and the Isles of Scilly, and ones I find myself teaching again and again. Likewise, I've gone for diversity, steering away from similar tangs to give you a unique tour of foraging in this region – one that is truly local. The results include leaves, shoots, flowers, fruits, seeds and seaweeds. Roots have been largely omitted due to legal issues (see Foraging Guidelines, page 9-10). Other plants have been left out because they are sparse, need a lot of processing, or can be harder to identify. Equally, I have chosen to leave out mushrooms and fungi, as they are increasingly seen as a specialist area, and require a specific introduction and finely honed skills.

Gorse and heather on the Cornish coast (above).
The author foraging gorse flowers (right)

One plant unique to Scilly is covered (Bermuda Buttercup), as is one rarely if ever found on Scilly, though it is common along the coast of Cornwall (Black Mustard). Blackthorn is included as it is abundant in Cornwall, though very sparse (so you are not encouraged to pick it) on Scilly. Other plants, such as Elder and Hawthorn, have been left out as they are common in Cornwall though not on Scilly and are covered in many other books. Similarly, plenty more edible plants found in Cornwall and Scilly can also be found across the UK. Hence my somewhat subjective choice.

About this Book

This book offers an accessible introduction to foraging in Cornwall and the Scillies. It covers plants and seaweeds that are easy to find and pick, so no special tools, hunting or fishing skills are required! It's for anyone who enjoys a walk; for those gentle ambles or even stumbles upon a beach, rockpool, coast path, or the glorious countryside. It seeks to inspire, not to overwhelm, with the what, where, how, why and when of wild food foraging in Cornwall and the Scillies.

It is both an identification guide and a recipe book. Plants and seaweeds are listed in alphabetical order; the seasonal chart on page 8 gives an idea of when to find specific parts of a plant. Identification is the key to successful foraging, so there is a detailed description and photograph of each plant and seaweed – in different seasons where applicable. However, if you are still in doubt, don't pick – the plant will return in future years, giving you further opportunities to forage safely. For each wild food, there is a step-by-step recipe, and suggested recipes and uses. Do experiment with suggestions that appeal to you; the ways to use wild foods are pretty much infinite, bringing out different flavours each time. Sometimes, all that is required of an existing recipe is replacing one ingredient with a wild one. However, tips for processing some foods are well worth noting, as are complementary flavours, because the wild ancestors of our cultivated foods sometimes need a little more attention in the kitchen.

Medicinal and nutritional qualities of each plant and seaweed are given, where known. Some of this information comes from scientific research; some from oral traditions, and observation over thousands of years of use by communities with different cultural traditions. I have extracted proven or consistent knowledge, cross-referencing sources to test the legitimacy of each claim. I have also included interesting anecdotes. All information is considered accurate at the time of publication. You will naturally favour some wild foods over others, but I recommend you persevere with a few that are less familiar, or hold less appeal, trying them from different growing spots, in different seasons and times of your life. Taste buds and wild foods can change, as can your relationship with foraging.

Seasonal Chart

A guide to the best picking times, based on nutrition and freshness. (Approximate times.)

Wild Food	Jan	Feb	Mar	Apr	May	Jun	Jul	Aug	Sep	Oct	Nov	Dec
Alexanders	L, SH	L, SH	L, ST	L, ST	L, ST, FL			S	S	S	L, S, ST	L, S, ST
Bermuda Buttercup	L	L	FL, ST	FL, ST	L, FL	L	L	L	L	L	L	L
Black Mustard	L	L	L	L	FL, L	FL	FL, S	S	S	S	L	L
Blackthorn			FL	FL	FL			F	F	F	F	
Bramble			L, ST	L, ST	L, ST	L		L, F	F	F		
Carrageen	FR	FR	FR	FR	FR	FR	FR	FR	FR	FR	FR	FR
Carrot (Wild)			L	L	L	FL	FL	S	S	S	S	S
Fennel	L	L	L	L	L	L	FL	FL, S	FL, S	S	S	
Gorse	FL	FL	FL	FL	FL	FL	FL	FL	FL	FL	FL	FL
Gutweed	FR	FR	FR	FR	FR	FR	FR	FR	FR	FR	FR	FR
Kelp	FR	FR	FR	FR	FR	FR	FR	FR	FR	FR	FR	
Nettle (Stinging)	L	L	L	L	L			L	L	L	L	L
Pennywort	L	L	L	L	L	L	L		L	L	L	L
Pepper Dulse	FR	FR	FR	FR	FR	FR	FR	FR	FR	FR	FR	FR
Rock Samphire			L	L	L	FL, L	FL	FL, S	S			
Sea Beet/Spinach	L	L	L	L	L	L			L	L	L	L
Sea Lettuce	FR	FR	FR	FR	FR	FR	FR	FR	FR	FR	FR	FR
Sea Radish	L	L	L	L	L	L, FL	L, FL, S		S, L	L	L	L
Sea Sandwort			L, SH	L, SH	L, SH	L, SH	L, SH	L, SH	L, SH	L, SH	L, SH	
Sorrel (Common)	L	L	L	L	L	L	F L	F L	L	L	L	L
Three-cornered Leek	SH, ST	SH, ST, L	L, ST	L, ST	L, ST, FL						SH, ST	SH, ST

Key: FL = flowers; FR = fronds; L = leaves; S = seeds; SH = shoots; ST = stems

Foraging Guidelines, Safety and Sustainability

Personally, I believe we should all have the right to forage as freely as the birds, animals and sea creatures. Contrary to fears of over-picking and damage, I feel that foraging offers exciting opportunities for hands-on learning which, in my experience, can naturally foster a sense of connection to and care for our environment. Nevertheless, due to our growing population, potential human greed, and other significant issues such as protection of certain species (whether plant or animal), it is worth highlighting some sensible as well as legal guidelines. Furthermore, some plants can make you sick and, in the worst-case scenario, be fatal. So I recommend following strictly the identification notes (*Get the ID right!*) and, once you are sure you have the right plant, taking precautions, such as eating small amounts of a new plant to check if you have a reaction – though this is no more likely than with cultivated plants. Similarly, some plants are not compatible with specific medications and can aggravate certain health conditions – *please seek medical advice where appropriate*. At the very least, please take note of the medicinal and nutritional qualities listed for each plant. If you truly want to enjoy foraging, then the following pointers should help you know, as well as increasing the chances, not only for you but for others, of being able to continue to forage in the future

- If unsure, don't pick the plant; check with an expert or cross-reference with books.

Foraging Guidelines and the Law

- Think tasters rather than harvesting (leaving enough for wildlife to feed).
- Only pick where there is an abundance and, it is advisable, never more than 30 percent of foliage or 20 percent of seeds or flowers, and only a very little, if at all, of flowers of annual plants (those that live for less than a year).

The author foraging on the beach (left). Seaweeds at Prussia Cove (right)

- Consider using scissors to help you take just the parts you want – including when picking seaweeds – as pulling can uproot and kill the plant.
- It is illegal to dig up roots without permission from the landowner.
- Respect local wildlife; stick to paths and rights of way, or at least stray sensitively.
- Pick away from sources of pollution, including pesticides; above dog-pee level, and only on clean, out-of-town beaches/ shoreline.
- Never pick rare plants (no plants listed in this book are rare).

- Always seek permission from the landowner, follow conservation laws, and avoid picking in protected areas such as Sites of Special Scientific Interest (SSSI).
- Pick for personal use only. In particular, you need a licence to forage seaweeds commercially.
- Take just what you need and leave the rest; vary picking sites, and leave areas as undisturbed as possible.
- Think about cultivating a wild patch in your own garden or yard, offering to weed (for food) friends' or neighbours' patches, and buying or harvesting a few wild seeds to grow at home.

Notes for the Cook

Cooking with foraged ingredients may take more preparation time, so be as relaxed as possible, include helping hands, and take your time to enjoy this age-old process of preparing and cooking.

Adapting recipes, and gluten/wheat/dairy/sugar-free diets

Feel free to adapt recipes. I have successfully substituted dairy products with sunflower oil or soya milk-substitutes, wheat with gluten-free flours, and sugar with fructose (fruit sugar) or honey.

Local ingredients

Cornwall and the Scillies have many producers of high-quality local ingredients. Please support them at Farmers' and Country markets, farm shops, homemade stalls, delicatessens, and some local-orientated stores. Products include sea salt, fish, seafood, eggs, cheeses, butter, cream and milk, meats, chicken and game, honey, flour, bread, and chocolate.

Conversions

All measurements are metric. Oven temperatures are for conventional electric ovens. Here are some equivalents:

Oven temperatures

160°C/fan 180°C/325°F/gas 3

175°C/fan 195°C°/325°F/gas 4

180°C/fan 200°C/350°F/gas 4

200°C/fan 220°C/400°F/gas 6

Metric/imperial

90ml	3 fl oz/5 tbsp
125ml	4 fl oz/7 tbsp
150ml	¼ pint
250ml	9 fl oz
300ml	10½ fl oz/½ pint
1 litre	1¾ pints
2 litres	3½ pints

Weight

5ml	1 tsp
10ml	1 dessert spoon
15ml	1 tbsp
8g	¼oz
25g	1oz
60g	2oz
120g	4oz
150g	5oz
175g	6oz
200g	7oz
350g	12oz/¾lb
440g	1lb
500g	1lb 2oz
600g	1lb 5oz
680g	1½ lb
1kg	2lb 3oz

Length

7cm	2¾ in
75cm	30 in
1m	39 in /3¼ ft
2m	78¾ in / 6½ ft

Alexanders — *Smyrnium olusatrum*

Where	Coastal and hedgerow, Cornwall, IOS
How abundant	Very
Edible parts	Leaves, young stems, larger stems peeled, seeds, flower buds, roots (but see page 10)
Season	Winter (leaves, young stems), spring (larger stems), late summer/autumn (seeds)
Nutrition/ medicinal	Considered to be high in vitamins and minerals, including vitamin C and potassium. Seeds contain protein, carbohydrates and oils; historically, the plant was used to stave off scurvy. Avoid if you have an allergy to celery.

Originally brought over by the Romans, now often considered an invasive. Best cooked, especially the large stems, peeled — it took me years to realize that!

Get the ID right!

- Hairless plant, grows to 1.25m
- Leaves dark green and glossy with toothed edge, stems and leaves grow in threes
- Flowers greeny-yellow, umbelliferous (umbrella-like)
- Stems ribbed, maybe purple/reddish stripes
- Seeds three-dimensional, ridged, black, sometimes with a whitish tinge

Suggested recipes and uses

Steam leaves and young stems as a side vegetable. Add to Spanish omelette, or cook in a creamy soup. Peel larger stems and cook like asparagus. Boil stems, using the liquid as stock for risottos (pages 14–15) or rice pudding. Grind seeds and add to bread, savoury or sweet biscuits. Simmer foliage or seeds with half their weight of sugar to make syrup; strain and use on desserts, in sorbet or ice-cream.

Tips

Late spring use large stems for stock (too fibrous to use as a vegetable). Store seeds by lightly dry-roasting; keep in dry, sterilized containers for up to two years.

Alexanders Risotto

A wonderfully aromatic dish with a subtle, wild twist.

Peel the stalks with a vegetable peeler or sharp knife* and cut into pieces, putting aside one large handful of the feathery foliage for the garnish. Put oil, half the butter and the onion in a pan, and sauté until golden. Add the sliced Alexanders, cover with stock and cook, covered, for approximately 15 minutes until very soft. Mash or blend; keep hot.

Heat remaining butter in a large saucepan.

When the foam begins to subside, mix in the rice and stir to coat the grains thoroughly. Sauté for a couple of minutes until the rice is slightly translucent. Turn up the heat, add the wine and let it bubble away, stirring the rice constantly. Now begin to add the stock, a ladleful at a time. When the liquid has been absorbed, add the next ladleful, stirring constantly and adjusting the heat accordingly. Halfway through cooking the rice, stir in the mashed Alexanders with all the juices. If you run out of stock before the rice is cooked, add boiling water and continue the cooking. When the rice is *al dente*, take the pan off the heat, add the cream (if using), Parmesan and plenty of black pepper. Mix well and keep the lid on until ready to serve. Garnish each portion with chopped Alexanders leaves.

If too fibrous, peel what you can, cook and blend, or cook whole, mash, then strain and use the liquid only.

Bermuda Buttercup — *Oxalis pes-caprae*

Where	Hedgerows and fields, IOS
How abundant	Fairly, in certain areas
Edible parts	Flowers, stalks, leaves
Season	Spring/early summer (flowers), rest of the year (foliage)
Nutrition/ medicinal	Good source of vitamin C. Contains oxalic acid, use sparingly. Not suitable for those susceptible to calcium oxolate kidney stones

Get the ID right!
- Clover-like leaves, hairless (in threes, heart-shaped)
- Plant grows up to 30cm tall
- Pale yellow flowers, large, floppy

Suggested recipes and uses
Use as with sorrel, though better visually, just in salad (pages 18–19), or as a garnish.

Tips
It is easiest to identify this plant when it is in flower as a few other plants also have clover-like leaves.

This bright yellow flower is like a breath of fresh air in the Scilly landscape. Locally considered a weed, it's neither a true buttercup (buttercups are poisonous, by the way), nor from Bermuda. Native to South Africa, the leaves remind me of wood sorrel (another member of the oxalis family), which gives a clue to its flavour – a citrus, tart tang.

Scilly Wild Spring Salad, Orange and Beetroot

Ingredients (quantities to suit)

Salad
- A scattering of wilds (e.g. sea sandwort, Bermuda buttercup, three-cornered leek flowers and stems; *photo also shows* chickweed, mallow and borage flowers)
- Slices of orange
- Diced cooked beetroot
- Cultivated leaves (optional)

Dressing
- 3 parts light oil (safflower, canola or soyabean)
- 1 part balsamic vinegar
- Sea salt and black pepper to taste

Visually satisfying, with a range of tastes and textures. Gather on a walk; make in moments.

Wash the leaves; check the flowers for sand or insects (washing makes them go limp and lose their nectar). Arrange all the salad ingredients in a bowl. Mix the dressing and just sprinkle it on, to enjoy the flavour of each plant. Serve immediately as a starter or side salad.

Black Mustard — *Brassica nigra*

Where	Coastal, Cornwall
How abundant	Very, where found. Rare, if at all, on IOS
Edible parts	Leaves, flowers, seeds
Season	Winter and spring (leaves); summer/autumn (flowers, seeds)
Nutrition/medicinal	Mustard seeds used to be crushed and put on the chest for colds, bronchial infections and rheumatic pains. They contain omega 3 and 6 fatty acids, potassium, calcium, phosphorous

One of the most powerful flavours in the Cornish hedgerow. Surprisingly hot and spicy!

Get the ID right!
- Grows to 2m tall, dark green leaves with slightly lighter stems, sometimes purple tinges where branches connect
- Lower, larger leaves, irregularly shaped, rough to touch (like sandpaper), with a jagged edge. The roughness is created by the raised hairs. Upper leaves can be simpler in shape and smooth
- Flowers are in balls of bright yellow, each having four petals (characteristic of the brassica/cabbage family)
- Seed pods long and thin, growing parallel to the stem

Suggested recipes and uses
Tear or shred the leaves and use in salad, sushi or sandwiches, as a garnish with meat, fish or vegetarian dishes. Use in mashed potatoes (pages 22–23).

Tips
Harvesting seeds is time-consuming, so using the foliage is best. Ideally used fresh and raw. Blanch only, as cooking thoroughly will remove the spiciness and the leaves will become like a cooked cabbage leaf.

Beef Stew with Black Mustard Mash

Ingredients (serves 4–5)

Beef stew
- 30ml extra virgin olive oil
- 440g onions, sliced
- 4 medium carrots, sliced
- 1kg stewing beef, trimmed and diced
- 10g plain flour
- 125ml sloe gin, or full-bodied red wine
- 125ml beef stock
- 150ml tomato purée
- Sea salt and black pepper to taste
- 220g mushrooms
- 60g nettle tops, washed
- 25g butter

Black mustard mash
- 680g potatoes, peeled
- Water, to cover the potatoes
- Splash of milk
- Knob of butter
- Sea salt and black pepper to taste
- 4–6 small, tender black mustard leaves
- Black mustard flowers to decorate (if in season)

A warming hearty dish.

For the beef stew: Preheat the oven to 160°C. Heat the olive oil in a large casserole dish, add the onions and carrots and sweat with the lid on for 10 minutes. Turn up the heat, add the beef and make sure each side is seared to seal the juices. Reduce the heat, stir in the flour and cook for 1 minute. Mix the wine or sloe gin, beef stock and tomato purée and gradually add to the dish, stirring as you go. Add salt and pepper, cover and cook in the oven for 2½–3 hours.

Meanwhile, sauté the mushrooms in a frying pan in butter. About 30 minutes before the dish is ready, add to the beef along with the washed nettle tops.

For the black mustard mash: Chop the potatoes, put them in a large pan, cover with water, bring to the boil and simmer for about 20 minutes, or until tender. Strain, add the milk, butter, salt and pepper to taste. Mash well. Just before serving, finely shred the black mustard leaves and mix in thoroughly.

Serve together, decorating the mashed potato with a few mustard flowers if available.

Blackthorn/Sloe — *Prunus spinosa*

Where	Woods, hedgerows right up to sea cliffs
How abundant	Common in hedgerows, rare on IOS
Edible parts	Fruits
Season	Late summer, autumn
Nutrition/ medicinal	Contains tannins, organic acids, sugars and vitamin C, diuretic, and considered of use for kidneys, bladder and stomach

I love to see blackthorn flowers in spring — a haze of white lining hedgerows and coastal paths.

Get the ID right!

- Stiff, thorny shrub, grows up to 4m; white flowers appear before the leaves in early spring
- Leaves matt and oval, coming into a pointed tip, with a slightly toothed edge
- Purplish fruits, like very small plums (about 1cm diameter) with a large stone inside

Suggested recipes and uses

For jams and sauces, use half sloes to apples, sieving out stones. Can be used with blackberries and hawthorn berries for meat gravies, and are good in venison or beef stew. Add with other wild fruits to fruit vinegar. Destone and use alcohol-soaked fruits for fruit compote, in trifle, or in chocolate (pages 26–27).

Tips

The spines of blackthorn are very sharp, and wounds from these thorns can often go septic, so picking carefully and with gloves is advised. Freezing the fruits (to mimic the first frost) helps sweeten them and means you don't need to prick each fruit with a fork when using to make a liqueur.

Sloe Liqueur and Sloe Liqueur Chocolates

To enjoy these chocolates, you first need to make sloe liqueur, and wait patiently for two to three months. It's worth it, for as well as homemade liqueur, you get this divine after-dinner treat.

For the sloe gin or vodka: Empty the bottle of alcohol – safely putting the contents aside – and half fill the bottle with the fruits. Once half full, use a funnel or carefully pour in the sugar until the fruits are completely covered. Fill the rest of the bottle with the alcohol. If you have a spare bottle you can repeat with the remaining ingredients. Leave for at least two months before drinking – can be left for up to a year, or more – shaking regularly or when you remember. Serve alone, with soda water, extra gin and crushed fruits, or with hot water for a hot toddy.

For the chocolates: Prepare moulds – either a mini-muffin baking tray lined with microwave-proof cling film, or silica moulds suitable for chocolates. Break the chocolate into pieces and melt in a heatproof bowl, nestled over a saucepan of simmering water on a low heat. The bowl should sit on top

Ingredients (quantities to suit)

Sloe gin or vodka
- Bottle of gin or vodka
- Sloes (picked after first frost, or defrosted and thawed from the freezer) – enough to half-fill a bottle
- Unrefined sugar – enough to cover fruits

Sloe liqueur chocolates
- 150g dark chocolate, at least 70% cocoa
- 40g destoned gin- or vodka-soaked sloes (*soaked for at least 2 months*)

of the saucepan rim, not in the simmering water. Ensure that the saucepan does not boil dry. Allow the chocolate to melt, do not overheat or stir. Meanwhile, chop the soaked sloes, and when the chocolate has melted, remove immediately from the heat and stir in the fruits. You could put some fruits, and/or a dash of sloe liqueur into each mould base first if you wish. Spoon the chocolate mixture into your moulds and leave to set in a cool place (can take from 15 minutes to 2 hours). When set, remove from moulds and eat within two weeks.

Bramble/Blackberry –

Rubus fruticosus agg.

Where	Hedgerows, wasteland, moorland, Cornwall, IOS
How abundant	Very
Edible parts	Fruits, young leaves, leaf buds, larger leaves, stems
Season	Early spring/summer (leaves and stems), late summer/autumn (fruits)
Nutrition/ medicinal	Rich in vitamin C, and the fruits are rich in fibre and contain sugars and pectin. Leaves have antiseptic, anti-fungal properties, and are good for upset stomachs, colds and flu

Get the ID right!

- Thick, spiny stems that spread up to 3m, and root when they touch the ground
- Toothed, oval leaves that come into a point, with prickles on back of leaf spines
- White or pink flowers
- Red, bulbous fruits that blacken when ripe

Suggested recipes and uses

For jam, use fruit alone, with apple or other wild fruits, using same weight fruit to sugar. Jelly and syrups can be made from leaves, stems or fruits (strain through a jelly bag), using half sugar to amount of liquid – serve with desserts or meat. Excellent in fruit vinegars; use fruits or leaves in herbal tea infusions and salads, or fruits in sweet baking (pages 30–31).

Blackberrying – going out with pots, bags or baskets to collect this wild fruit – seems to be the one kind of fruit foraging that most Britons have done.

Tips

There are, or were, up to 200 varieties of brambles, all with a slightly different taste, so if you find a good patch, you may wish to return to it!

Jammy Blackberry Muffins

So much is written about super fruits, yet the humble blackberry is just as good nutritionally and taste-wise as many of them. As these moreish muffins will show.

For the jam: First make the jam by heating the sugar and fruits, stirring all the time, so that they do not stick to the pan or burn. Bring them to the boil, simmer and stir for 40 minutes.* Put aside and allow to cool, at least a little. When cooler, the jam should thicken more.

* Most jam recipes give a setting test. This one doesn't because, with the long cooking time, it does set.

For the muffins: Preheat the oven to 180°C. Grease a muffin tin, or line a tin with paper cases. Sieve flour and baking powder into a bowl, add sugar and set aside. Beat the eggs well in another bowl, then add the milk and melted butter. Add the wet ingredients to the dry ones, then add the blackberries. Stir well, though do not over beat.

Ingredients (makes 12)

Jammy filling
- 100g unrefined sugar
- 100g blackberries

Muffins
- Butter for greasing
- 200g plain flour
- 10ml baking powder
- 50g unrefined sugar
- 2 eggs
- 175ml milk
- 50g melted butter
- 100g blackberries
- Crème fraîche to serve (optional)

Half-fill each cake hole with cake mixture, add a teaspoon of jam, and a dollop of cake mixture on top. Fill to the top if small cases, or two-thirds full if using larger cases. Bake in the oven for approximately 20–25 minutes, until golden brown. Remove and cool. Eat as a snack, or serve with crème fraîche.

Carrageen/Irish Moss and Stackhouse
— *Chondrus crispus* and *Gigartina stellata*

Where	Rock pools or lower shore, Cornwall, IOS
How abundant	Very, in specific areas
Edible parts	Foliage
Season	All year round
Nutrition/ medicinal	Considered almost a complete food, due to balance of protein, carbohydrate and fats, good trace of vitamins and minerals, particularly calcium. *Gigartina stellata* is high in vitamin C. Traditionally eaten when sick to aid health, and proven to be of benefit against cold viruses

Get the ID Right!

- Usually up to 15cm tall/wide
- Flat, wide fronds with no mid-rib or channel, branching into two, then two, etc
- Red to purple in colour, sometimes olive green from sun exposure, or pink to white if found dried; if submerged, the frond tips can shine iridescent in bright light
- A variation is *Gigartina stellata* (Stackhouse), whose fronds curl in slightly at the edges; the fruiting bodies (*facing page below*) appear as small bumps on older plants

Suggested recipes and uses

Both seaweeds will set dishes like smoked mackerel mousse, panna cotta (pages 34–35), jellies or ice-cream. Alternatively use them sparingly to dissolve into and thicken soups.

Tips

When heated, this seaweed sets and thickens liquids, and has been used in many processed foods. Here you'll be able to use the pure ingredient.

Always cut seaweeds, keeping the base root intact so it can continue growing in its found location. Gives a mild 'taste of the sea' which needs to be balanced with other flavours.

White Chocolate Panna Cotta

Ingredients (serves 4)

- 30g fresh carrageen, rinsed thoroughly (or 8g dried)
- 25g unrefined sugar
- 250ml whole milk
- 300ml water
- 150ml double cream
- 100g white cooking chocolate, in pieces
- Fruits to decorate (optional; *photo* physalis)

Impressive, easy and decadent!

Put the carrageen, sugar, milk and water in a saucepan. Simmer for 20 minutes. Strain through a fine sieve or jelly bag, and return to the heat with the cream and chocolate. Bring to an almost simmer – watch carefully – until it starts to quiver. Take off the heat and stir well, ensuring the chocolate is fully melted and well combined. Pour into ramekins or chocolate moulds and set in the fridge (2–5 hours). Serve in the dishes, or sit them in warm water and carefully cut around the edge to loosen and remove. Serve alone or with tart fruits/fruit sauce.

Carrot (Wild) — *Daucus carota*

Where	Coastal, cliffs right down to beach edges, Cornwall and IOS
How abundant	Very, in specific areas
Edible parts	Flowers, seeds, roots (but see page 10), leaves
Season	Spring to autumn (flowers), late summer (seeds), autumn/winter (roots), all year round (leaves/greenery)
Nutrition/ medicinal	Good for digestive ailments, contains vitamin B complex, sugars and pectins. Infusions can counter cystitis and kidney stones, and reputedly increase levels of sex hormones. **Seeds can be abortive and should not be digested if pregnant or trying to get pregnant**

Get the ID right!
- Grows up to 75cm tall (though often smaller), with a stout, rough, hairy stem
- Flowers are umbelliferous (umbrella-like), with long, small leaves coming down direct from the base of the flower head
- Flowers can be white, white with a single pink/red flower in the middle, mottled white and pink, or completely pink
- Leaves feathery, similar to cultivated carrot

Suggested recipes and uses

Seeds to flavour cakes, biscuits (pages 38–39), sorbets, ice-cream, bread, soups, dhal or toast, and added to salads. Flowers and green parts can be infused for subtle-tasting syrups.

Tips

The roots are very fibrous, so flowers or seeds are preferable. For older foliage, you'll need to simmer to release the flavour (10–60 minutes). Use seeds whole – either fresh or dried – from the stem, as the flavour is released when bitten into.

One of the prettiest coastal flowers I know, so I'm often reluctant to pick it. Despite being the origin of our cultivated carrots, its taste is surprisingly aromatic.

Honey and Carrot Seed Cookies

A wholesome, rustic biscuit with a comforting flavour.

Preheat the oven to 175°C. Heat the honey and butter slowly in a saucepan until melted, then take off the heat. Mix all the dry ingredients together in a bowl, then add slowly to the honey and butter, mixing thoroughly. The mixture should be sticky and stiff.

Grease a baking tray. Shape the mixture into balls (you may need a little extra flour for this) and place on the baking tray about 5cm apart. Flatten them into cookie-like shapes, and bake for 20–25 minutes, or until golden.

Enjoy on their own or with a warm drink!

Fennel — *Foeniculum vulgare*

Where	Coastal Cornwall, IOS
How abundant	Varies, common in places
Edible parts	Leaves, flowers, seeds
Season	Spring/early summer (leaves), summer/early autumn (flowers/seeds)
Nutrition/ medicinal	A digestive aid, helps to break down fatty foods, used to assist slimming. Reduces bloating and can be helpful for menstrual pains. Has proved to increase milk flow in breastfeeding mums

Get the ID right!

- Grows up to 1.2m high, hairless stems which are hollow when old
- Feathery leaves similar to dill, pale grey-green in colour
- Flowers are yellow, umbelliferous (umbrella-like), and scent is of fresh aniseed
- Seeds are grey-green to brown, depending on how fresh

Suggested recipes and uses

Chop and mix leaves with butter for a herb butter. Add to salads, bake with fish, use in risotto, omelettes or similar. Make tempura with the flower heads, grind seeds into bread, sweet biscuits, or savoury dishes. Also good as a tea, or in desserts such as sorbet (pages 42–43).

Tips

The roots of wild fennel are different from the cultivated kind. With the wild one, use only the aerial parts.

With a refreshing aniseed flavour, fennel is great with savoury or sweet dishes, and its medicinal qualities are excellent.

Fennel Flower Fritters and Fennel Leaf Sorbet

Ingredients (serves 4)

Sorbet
• 30g fennel foliage (leaf and small stalks)
• 240ml water
• 80g sugar

Fritters
• 200ml cold milk
• 1 large egg, beaten
• 90g sifted plain flour
• Sunflower oil for frying
• Icing sugar to decorate (optional)
• 2–3 fennel flower heads per person (stalk remaining – to hold on to when frying)

An aniseed delight of differing textures.

For the sorbet: Wash and chop the fennel, place in a large heat-proof bowl and pour on 150ml of boiling water. Cover and leave overnight. Meanwhile, in a small saucepan add the sugar to 90ml of water, stir and bring to the boil before leaving to cool. When the infused fennel is ready, blend it in a food blender before straining it through a fine sieve, squeezing until all the liquid is removed.

Mix the sugar syrup with the infused liquid and churn in an ice-cream maker or place in ice-lolly moulds. Alternatively, transfer to a metal baking tin and place in the freezer, stirring with a fork every half an hour until frozen, smooth and creamy. Freeze until required.

For the fritters: Pour the milk into a mixing bowl, mix in the beaten egg, add the flour and roughly fold in with a fork. Do not beat, as the batter should be lumpy.

Heat the oil in a wok or a frying pan with 1–2 cm of oil. When hot, hold flower heads by the stalk, wipe them through the batter to cover, and fry gently in the oil until golden brown. Remove from the oil and drain on paper towel.

To serve, snip the main stalk off each flower, and enjoy warm or cold with fennel sorbet and a dusting of icing sugar.

Gorse — *Ulex europaeus* or *Ulex gallii*

Where	Moorland, heaths, coast, Cornwall, IOS
How abundant	Very, where found
Edible parts	Flowers
Season	Spring (young shoots), all year round, though mostly spring and summer (flowers)
Nutrition/ medicinal	In Bach Flower Remedies and homeopathy, gorse is said to counter 'hopelessness and despair'. Young shoots have been used as a nutritious fodder for horses and cattle

The bright yellow of gorse flowers is an uplifting sight in winter, or a hazy moorland view at other times.

Get the ID right!
- Evergreen shrub, grows to 1.5–2m high
- Spiky foliage, bright yellow flowers with a coconut scent
- Furry seed pods that you can hear pop open in late summer
- Common gorse (*Ulex europaeus*) flowers in spring/early summer. It is larger than Western gorse (*U. gallii*), and the latter – or a hybrid of the two – flowers the rest of the year

Suggested recipes and uses
Infusions for tea, flower syrups, sorbet, ice-cream, custard or macaroons, or use in rice pudding (pages 46–47). Decorate salads or creamy coconut curries. Make wine from the flowers, or pickle the buds and add to salads.

Tips
The spikes are sharp, so pick flowers with gloves on, and in full sun to capture their scent. Dried flowers (page 45) have a more intense scent for flavouring foods. This plant can smell strongly of coconut, but the scent in cooking and eating is fainter and more floral.

Gorse Flower Rice Pudding

Ingredients (serves 4)

Pudding
- 50g fresh gorse flowers
- 1.3 litres full fat milk
- 100g pudding or risotto rice
- 50g unrefined sugar
- 25g butter

Syrup
- 16g dried gorse flowers, or 20–25g semi-dried flowers
- 75g unrefined sugar
- Water, to cover flowers and sugar

A delicately perfumed dish, enhanced greatly by the addition of gorse syrup.

To dry flowers for the syrup: Spread out freshly picked flowers in the sun or a warm place for 48 hours, or dry in the oven at the lowest temperature for 2–4 hours. Semi-dried flowers are also fine.

For the pudding: Preheat the oven to 180°C. Simmer the fresh gorse flowers in milk for 15 minutes, then blend with a food blender to help break up the flower pods. Meanwhile, put the rice, sugar and butter in an ovenproof dish and pour on the infused milk. Bake in the oven for 1–2 hours, or until all the milk is absorbed and the rice is soft and cooked. There will be a cooked, milky skin over the dish.

For the syrup: While the pudding is baking, prepare the syrup by placing the dried or semi-dried gorse flowers and sugar in a pan and just covering with hot water. Simmer for 10 minutes before straining through a fine sieve or muslin cloth, making sure you get every last drop.

Serve the rice pudding hot with generous spoonfuls of syrup over each portion.

Gutweed – *Ulva/Enteromorpha intestinalis*

Where	Rockpools, Cornwall and IOS, likes nutrient-rich areas
How abundant	Very
Edible parts	Whole, though cut so as not to uproot
Season	All year round, best in spring
Nutrition/ medicinal	Up to 18 percent protein. High in vitamin C, contains a wide range of other vitamins, including B12, and minerals including calcium, iron, magnesium and manganese

Get the ID right!
- Grows up to 50cm long, single bright green strands with no branches
- The strands are actually tubes, reminiscent of intestines, which inflate to bring the weed to the surface of the water
- Strands can vary in width, from fine to around 8 cm in breadth

Suggested recipes and uses
Use fresh or dried in salads. Generously as a herb in oatcakes, or deep fried as a side dish or garnish (pages 50–51).

Tips
Pick using scissors, to avoid uprooting the seaweed. Dried, it is a great, flavourful herb. Air-dry, or dry in the oven at a low temperature. Store in the dark, to keep its colour.

Drying seaweeds for frying
Fresh seaweed spits if fried wet. Prepare gutweed by washing thoroughly, discarding any that has sand inside its tubes. Semi-dry between two tea towels, squeezing out excess moisture and getting as dry as possible. If you have time, dry for several hours on the lowest temperature in the oven, or on a washing line on a hot summer's day.

A light, tender sea vegetable, which is widespread and easy to spot on beaches.

Crab Cakes, Crispy Seaweed and Wild Tartar Sauce

A classic dish with a few wild spins.

For the crab cakes: Boil the potatoes in a large pan for 15–20 minutes, or until tender. Drain, leave to steam dry for a few minutes, then return to the pan. Mash the potatoes with the crab meat, using a fork or potato masher. Add the lemon zest, onion or leek, and a third of the gutweed, finely chopped. Combine ingredients well, and add salt and pepper to taste. Mix in the egg yolk and divide the mixture into 16 portions, shaping each into a patty. Pop in the fridge, ideally for at least 4 hours, to firm up.

To cook the crab cakes, put a splash of olive oil into a large frying pan on a high heat. Add several patties, cook for 2 minutes on each side, or until golden and cooked through. Repeat, until all the patties are cooked. Place in a low temperature in the oven until ready to serve.

For the tartar sauce: Simply blend the sea sandwort with the mayonnaise in a food blender.

For the crispy seaweed: Once the crab cakes are ready, put a couple of pieces of kitchen towel on a plate. In a deep frying pan, heat about 1cm in depth of olive oil. When the oil is almost smoking, gently lower in small batches of the remaining gutweed and cook for 10 seconds. Remove, and place on the kitchen towel. Serve immediately with the crab cakes and tartar sauce.

Kelp — *Laminaria digitata*

Where	Low tide areas, off rocks, Cornwall, IOS
How abundant	Very
Edible parts	Fronds only, leave stem attached to the holdfast
Season	All year round, best in spring
Nutrition/ medicinal	Can stimulate taste buds, is high in iron, iodine and zinc, and good range of other minerals and vitamins. Rich in sodium alginate, which has been recorded to significantly reduce radioactive strontium absorption – i.e., effective antidote, of sorts, after exposure to radiation

The tree of the seascape, and a favourite playing environment for seals. Kelp is actually the family name for a range of seaweeds – all edible. *Laminaria digitata* is the most common of the kelps in Cornwall and IOS and perfect for this recipe.

Get the ID right!
- Grows to 1m or more in length
- A thick, smooth, leathery-feeling seaweed, with a thick stem and holdfast (equivalent of a root) and several fronds/branches coming from one stem
- Up to 15cm in breadth
- Olive-brown in colour

Suggested recipes and uses
Cook with pulses or lentils to reduce cooking time and flatulence. Simmer to make stock or soup (pages 54–55), slice and cook as noodles, cook with rice dishes or deep fry for kelp crisps.

Tips
Dry quickly (36 hours); store for up to a year. Pick the freshest growth (near the root, not the ends) – only a couple of fronds per plant.

Kelp, Miso and Ginger Soup

Ingredients (serves 4)

- Approx 2 x 1m strips fresh (200g) kelp (or 40g dried)
- 2 litres water
- 3 large flat mushrooms, chopped, or small handful of dried mushrooms
- 2cm chunk fresh ginger, chopped
- 1 medium carrot, diced
- 15ml olive oil
- 1 medium onion, sliced
- 1 clove garlic, chopped
- Three-cornered leek or spring onion to garnish (optional)
- 1–2 tbsp miso paste (dark or light) to taste
- Black pepper to taste

A nourishing, tasty soup. This recipe is based on a traditional Japanese recipe, in which kombu seaweed (the Japanese name for kelp) is used. Many Japanese seaweeds can be found in the waters surrounding Cornwall and the Scillies… it's just that we have British names for them!

Place the kelp in a saucepan, cover with water and simmer for 40–60 minutes. If using dried mushrooms, cut and add in also. In the last 15 minutes, add the ginger and carrot. Remove the kelp and finely slice about half of it (or more if you wish) into short, slim noodle sizes, and add more water to make up to 2 litres.

Meanwhile, in a frying pan heat the oil and fry the onion for a couple of minutes, then add the garlic, before adding the mushrooms (if fresh ones). Stir until the onion is soft and the mushrooms cooked and juicy, then add to the cooked soup base. Chop the three-cornered leek or spring onion (if using) and sprinkle on top. Remove from the heat.

Put about 4 tablespoons of the liquid into a small bowl and thoroughly mix with the miso paste before returning to the pan. Adjust the taste with more miso and black pepper, if required.

Nettle (Stinging) — *Urtica dioica*

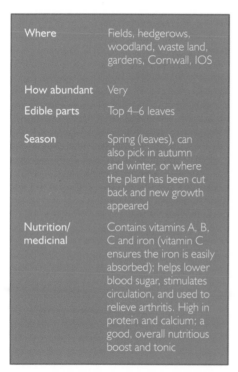

Where	Fields, hedgerows, woodland, waste land, gardens, Cornwall, IOS
How abundant	Very
Edible parts	Top 4–6 leaves
Season	Spring (leaves), can also pick in autumn and winter, or where the plant has been cut back and new growth appeared
Nutrition/ medicinal	Contains vitamins A, B, C and iron (vitamin C ensures the iron is easily absorbed); helps lower blood sugar, stimulates circulation, and used to relieve arthritis. High in protein and calcium; a good, overall nutritious boost and tonic

Remove the sting (by cooking), and this plant becomes a food to celebrate rather than a curse. May the feast begin!

Get the ID right!
- Grows up to 1m tall
- Oval, hairy, dark green leaves, deeply toothed and with a pointed tip
- The hairs (present all over the plant) sting, creating heat, itching and a throbbing pain for hours
- Flowers greenish, sometimes tinged purple, are like catkins, attached below the leaves and coming off the main stem

Suggested recipes and uses
Replace spinach with nettles in any recipe, for example, in pasta, gnocchi, or risotto. Great in nettle & potato curry and pesto. Nettle syrup and sorbet are also good. Combines well with lemon or ginger. The classics are nettle soup (pages 58–59) and nettle beer; the latter is a one-week wonder – takes four days to make, and often even less to drink!

Tips
Pick using thick gloves. Do not pick/eat when in flower (photo on right). Cooking for a couple of minutes will completely remove the sting.

Nettle Soup

Ingredients (serves 4)

- 15ml oil for frying
- 1 onion, peeled and sliced
- 2 celery stems, chopped (optional)
- 2 medium potatoes, peeled and chopped
- 500ml milk
- 500ml vegetable stock, hot
- 250g nettle tops, washed
- 4 cooked local sausages (optional), sliced
- Crème fraîche for garnish (optional)

A fresh adaption of an old Cornish recipe.

Heat the oil in a large pan, and when hot add the onion, lowering the heat and allowing to sweat with the lid on for 5 minutes. Add the celery, if using, and sweat for a further 5 minutes. Next, add the potatoes, milk and stock and bring to the boil, simmering for 10 minutes or until the potatoes are soft. Carefully add the nettle tops – either with gloves or two wooden spoons – and cook for a further 10 minutes. Blend in a food processor before adding the sliced sausages and crème fraiche, if using. Enjoy immediately.

Pennywort/Navelwort –

Umbilicus rupestris

Where	Stone walls, rocks and the base of tree trunks, Cornwall, IOS
How abundant	Very, less in IOS
Edible parts	Leaves and stem
Season	All year, when not in flower, best in spring
Nutrition/ medicinal	'Wort' = plant of worth. Used as a poultice to treat anything from piles, mild burns, scalds, chilblains to sore breasts. Considered a diuretic; useful internally for inflamed liver or spleen

A succulent thirst-quencher of the hedgerow.

The Cornish plaster *(Hatfield, see page 96.)*
The fine membrane of the pennywort plant used to be peeled off and put where a thorn or splinter was embedded under the skin. After a day or two, when the 'plaster' was removed, the thorn would be drawn out.

Get the ID right!
- Grows up to 50cm tall (when in flower)
- Leaves 1–4cm diameter (like old penny)
- Green, fleshy leaves, paler stem. Leaves dented in the middle like an inward belly button, or 'navel'; slightly scalloped edge
- Flower is pale green or pinkish-white and bell-shaped

Suggested recipes and uses
Best used whole in salads and garnishes or remove the stem and use as a canapé base (pages 62–63), or blended into drinks (mix with sugar syrup) or dips.

Tips
Use fresh, as these delicate plants are easily bruised and don't keep well once picked. Keep with stalks in water. The mild flavour varies from bitter to sweet, so try in different seasons, from different growing places.

Pennywort and Cream Cheese Canapés

Ingredients (serves 4)

- 16 large pennywort leaves (stalks snapped off and eaten or left in the hedgerow)
- 15g herbs – e.g. parsley, dill, chervil, tarragon, three-cornered leek, sorrel
- 150g creamy cheese – e.g. goat's cheese, not too crumbly, not too gooey

This recipe can almost be done with your eyes closed. Though with eyes open, the visual effect brings a smile to any dinner table.

Wash the pennyworts and gently pat dry with a cloth, or wipe or dust off any dirt or debris. Finely chop the herbs and mix with the cream cheese – I like to keep each herb separate, and use three, for variety. Using your fingers and a teaspoon, carefully place a ball of the cream cheese mix in the middle of each leaf. Serve as canapés or as a salad garnish.

Pepper Dulse –

Osmundea pinnatifida/Laurencia pinnatifida

Where	Rocks at low tide, sides, undersides or top, Cornwall, IOS
How abundant	Very, in places
Edible parts	Leaf/foliage
Season	All year round
Nutrition/ medicinal	Rich in minerals, including calcium, magnesium, iron, manganese, copper and zinc; up to 8 percent protein, low in fat, high in fibre

The small fern of the sea, and easily missed because of its size. Such an amazing flavour for such a small plant.

Get the ID right!

- 2–20cm in length (I've never seen it longer than about 8cm)
- Flat fronds that branch off the main stems
- Colours vary from brownish-purple to olive green

Suggested recipes and uses

Dry and use as stock for seafood dishes. Simmer with fish bones and heads to make your own tasty fish stock. Use fresh in dishes such as pasta with mussels (pages 66–67).

Tips

As this is a small seaweed, take particular care when picking. Cutting with scissors can be useful so as not to uproot and kill the whole weed. Traditionally, pepper dulse is dried and used as a spice (giving the flavour more depth); however, using it fresh means you can enjoy its texture and fresher, sharper flavours.

Pasta with Mussels and a Pepper Dulse Sauce

Ingredients (serves 4)

- 220g pasta shapes
- 15ml oil for frying
- 6 shallots, finely sliced
- 300ml dry white wine
- 20g fresh pepper dulse
  (or dried and rehydrated)
- Sea salt and black pepper to taste
- 1kg mussels (washed and bearded)
- 30g sorrel

Cornish mussels

Many fine companies grow and harvest nutritious mussels from Cornish waters, as has been the way for generations. If harvesting wild ones, there are some important things to remember. Ensure that the water quality that you're picking from is excellent; only pick mussels that are 51mm or more in length (a legal landing size), and only when there's an 'R' in the month (thus avoiding summer months when mussels breed and can become gritty, and when water-born bacteria is more likely to grow). And, of course, follow the notes to the right on mussels.

This dish has a wonderful taste of the sea. It is easy to put together, with seasoning that sings off the plate.

Cook the pasta according to the instructions on the packet. Drain and cover to keep warm.

Meanwhile, in a large, heavy-bottomed pan, heat the oil; lower the heat and gently fry the shallots for a couple of minutes. Add the white wine, pepper dulse, and salt and pepper to taste. Bring the white wine to the boil, add the mussels,* lower the heat and cover for 3–4 minutes, or until all the mussels have opened.

Just before serving, finely shred the sorrel and add it to the pan. Serve the pasta in broad, shallow bowls, and ladle over the mussels in sauce.

*Never use any mussels that are open before they go in the pan. Check they are alive by tapping open shells with the back of a knife. If they snap shut, you can use them. Discard any that do not open after cooking.

Rock Samphire – *Crithmum maritimum*

Where	Cliffs and rocks, occasionally in the sand, always above the high-tide mark, Cornwall, IOS
How abundant	Very, in places
Edible parts	Leaves and stems
Season	Late spring – in summer the flavour can be too strong
Nutrition/ medicinal	Rich in vitamin C and minerals, used as a digestive aid and apparently to help lose weight. High in omega-3 oils

Get the ID right!
- Grows up to 40cm in height, grey-green plant, hairless and slightly ribbed
- Fleshy, tubular stems and flattened leaves
- Yellow-tinged flowers, umbelliferous (umbrella-like), with bulbous seeds that come later
- Strong citrus/aromatic scent when crushed

Suggested recipes and uses
Cook for just 2–3 minutes, add to salads, use as a side vegetable with fish or seafood (pages 70–71). Good in risotto, stir fry, or serve with eggs, in feta cheese salad, or pickled with wedges of lemon and fennel seeds.

Tips
In summer the flavour can be too strong to use successfully.

The superior, both nutritionally and in taste, of the two samphires (the other is marsh samphire, which grows in salty estuaries). A wonderful lemony and aromatic flavour.

Pan-fried Mackerel and Rock Samphire with Crushed Coriander Seeds

Ingredients (serves 4)

- 1 tbsp coriander seeds
- Juice of 1 lemon
- 60ml extra virgin olive oil
- Sea salt and black pepper to taste
- 4 fresh mackerel, gutted, plus headed and tailed if you prefer
- 125g rock samphire
- Water, to cook the rock samphire
- Parsley to garnish (optional)

I like to serve this plant simply – allowing the flavours to speak for themselves.

Heat a frying pan (don't add oil) and dry fry the coriander seeds. They will be ready in a few minutes – when you start to smell their aroma – do not allow to burn.

Remove from the pan and roughly crush the seeds, using a pestle and mortar, or carefully under a rolling pin.

Mix the lemon juice with half the oil, the coriander seeds and a little salt. Put aside.

Next, heat the remaining oil in a good-sized frying pan.

Make sure the fish is quite dry (dry on a cloth if needed) before lowering into the pan. Cook for about 4 minutes on each side, or until the fish is easily coming off the bone.

Meanwhile, wash the rock samphire and heat a small amount of water (just 1cm in depth) in a medium-sized saucepan. When boiling, add the rock samphire, place a lid on top and cook for 2–3 minutes.

Strain off the liquid and serve immediately with the mackerel, the dressing, and garnish, if using.

Sea Beet/Spinach –

Beta vulgaris ssp. *maritima*

Where	Coastal areas, Cornwall, IOS
How abundant	Very, where found
Edible parts	Leaves and stem
Season	All year round, best in spring, then autumn and winter
Nutrition/ medicinal	Rich in vitamins C and A, and contains a range of minerals

Get the ID right!
- Bright green leaves taper down into a ribbed stem; stem occasionally red-striped
- Leaves are thick and glossy, and come into a spear shape
- When flowering, can trail to up to 80cm in length, with tiny flowers that may be white, green or red/pink

Suggested recipes and uses
As spinach – use as a side vegetable, in risotto or seafood dishes (pages 74–75). Best cooked, though the really young leaves can be used raw.

Tips
A naturally buttery flavour, which doesn't necessarily need oil or butter added. Wilts down just like spinach, despite its sometimes tough exterior. Some prefer to remove the main stalk, and just use the tender parts – I like to use it whole.

The mother and father of most cultivated beets, including spinach, beetroot and sugar beet. Keeps its shape beautifully when cooked.

Baked Lemon Sole with Fennel, New Potatoes and Sea Beet

Ingredients (serves 4)

- 4 sprigs fennel leaves
- 10 three-cornered leek stems (or 1 bunch spring onions)
- Juice of 1 lemon
- 45ml extra virgin olive oil
- Sea salt and black pepper to taste
- 4 good-sized lemon sole (filleted, or tail, head and side bones removed if preferred)
- 700g salad potatoes
- 300g sea beet
- Water, to cook the sea beet

Fish, potatoes and wild greens – perfect!

Preheat the oven to 200°C and cut four pieces of baking paper or foil, large enough to wrap each fish on all four sides and contain the juices.

To prepare the dressing, roughly chop the fennel leaves and young stems, three-cornered leeks or spring onions and mix with the lemon juice, olive oil, salt and pepper. Place each fish in the centre of a piece of baking paper or foil, spoon a quarter of the dressing over each fish, wrap and place on a baking tray.

Next, prepare the potatoes by ensuring they're all of similar size, cutting in half if necessary. Wash the sea beet, and remove any really tough stems – keeping the rest of the leaves and stems whole. Bake the fish for 15 minutes.

Meanwhile, put the potatoes in a pan of cold water, cover and bring to the boil. Once boiling, reduce to a simmer and cook for 15 minutes, or until firm though cooked through.

In the last 7 minutes, place the sea beet in a small saucepan, with a very little water and cook with the lid on for 5 minutes, or until the leaves and stems are tender. When the fish is ready, turn off the oven until the potatoes and sea beet are ready.

Plate up your fish, potatoes and sea beet, pouring over the remaining dressing.

Sea Lettuce — *Ulva lactuca*

Where	Rock pools and inter-tidal areas. Also salt marshes, Cornwall, IOS
How abundant	Very
Edible parts	All (cutting to leave holdfast attached to rock or source)
Season	Spring, though also good rest of the year
Nutrition/ medicinal	Good content of iron, vitamins A, B and C, protein and traces of a range of minerals

Get the ID right!
- A bright, light green sheet, sometimes wavy at the edges, up to 50cm in breadth or length, though often smaller
- Thin and smooth in texture, translucent

Suggested recipes and uses
Use in salads with Japanese rice wine or vinaigrette, in risotto, pan fry with fish, use in bread (pages 78–79), deep fry as a snack or side vegetable.

Tips
Always pick seaweeds fresh, still living and attached to rocks. The exception to this rule is directly after a storm, when seaweeds have only just detached, and therefore still remain fresh enough to eat.

The 'lettuce' of the sea. Versatile and tasty. Sea lettuce and gutweed (pages 48–49) are now considered to be in the same *Ulva* family, of which there are many sub-species. Despite the name 'lettuce', I find this seaweed a little tough to use raw, and prefer to fry or boil it lightly if using as a side vegetable.

Sea Lettuce and Wild Carrot Seed Bread

Ingredients (makes 1 loaf)

- 500g wholemeal flour
- Pinch of sea salt
- 5ml quick yeast
- Small handful dried sea lettuce, broken into pieces (more if you're using fresh)
- 15ml dried wild carrot seeds (optional)
- 10ml honey
- 400ml warm water
- 15ml olive oil

The sea lettuce adds a good taste and colour to this loaf. Great with soup, or for picnics.

Preheat the oven to 200°C. Put the flour, salt and yeast in a large mixing bowl and stir. Add the sea lettuce and carrot seeds. Dissolve the honey in the warm water and slowly add to the flour mix. Stir in, adding the oil. Knead for 10 minutes, then shape, and place on a greased baking tray, or in a greased, 1kg loaf tin. Cover with a clean cloth and leave in a warm place for 20 minutes, or until doubled in size. Bake in the oven for 40–45 minutes, or until hollow-sounding when tapped.

Sea Radish –

Raphanus raphanistrum ssp. *maritimus*

Where	Sandy soil, near the sea, Cornwall, IOS
How abundant	Very, in undisturbed areas
Edible parts	Leaves, stems, flowers, seed pods, roots (but see page 10)
Season	All year round, winter–spring (leaves); summer (flowers and seed pods)
Nutrition/ medicinal	Cultivated radishes* have good levels of copper, manganese and potassium, vitamins C and K, and contain calcium, magnesium, iron and zinc. They have anti-bacterial and anti-fungal properties, are useful for coughs, respiratory problems, digestive complaints and liver conditions * Little research has been carried out on the wild sea radish

Surprisingly spicy and radishy!

Get the ID right!
- Hairy plant, with rough lower leaves, grows in a rosette form at ground level, before becoming upright
- Leaves have ragged, toothed edge, that wave in and out from the stem, with smaller leaflets lower on the stem
- Stems, thick and juicy, flowers pale yellow, four petals (brassica – cabbage family)
- Bulbous seed pods, like beads

Suggested recipes and uses
Leaves fresh in pesto (use immediately), stems in stir fries, flowers raw in salads and garnishes. Leaves fried or raw (pages 82–83). Seed pods raw as a snack, in salads or pickled.

Tips
Only eat seed pods when young, otherwise they become too fibrous. Cooking this plant removes some of the heat, though it is definitely more versatile than black mustard.

Cod in Creamy Sauce with Crispy Wild Leaves

Ingredients (serves 4)

- 45ml olive oil for frying
- Mussel shells from about 1lb mussels (meat removed), or other empty shellfish, broken up
- 100ml dry white wine
- 2 cloves garlic, sliced
- 500ml double cream
- Handful Bermuda buttercup leaves, stems and flowers
- Sea salt and black pepper to taste
- 4 cod steaks (sustainably caught)
- Handful rock samphire
- 4 large, hand-size pieces sea lettuce
- 4 large leaves sea radish

Particularly good with both raw and crispy-fried sea radish leaves.

Heat 15ml of oil in a large saucepan, add the shellfish shells, sauté for 3 minutes, then add the wine, garlic and cream. Boil for 2 minutes and simmer for 20 minutes, or until reduced to half the amount of liquid. Meanwhile, chop the stems and leaves of the Bermuda buttercup, and in the last 5 minutes of cooking, add them to the saucepan.

Season with salt and pepper to taste. Strain the sauce through a sieve and put aside.

Heat the rest of the oil in a shallow frying pan, on a medium heat for about 3 minutes. Season the cod with salt and pepper, and fry the fish steaks for about 5 minutes on each side, turning carefully. They'll be ready when the fish breaks away easily when cut.

Meanwhile, wash all the rest of the leaves and the seaweed. Pat dry. Heat a little water in a small pan, and cook the rock samphire for 2 minutes. While the fish is still cooking, add the sea lettuce to the pan, and allow to cook for 2–3 minutes.

Finally, chop the sea radish leaves, and put half aside. Remove the fish and sea lettuce and keep them warm, then add the rest of the oil to the frying pan and allow to heat for 2–3 minutes, before frying half the sea radish leaves until crispy. Arrange each individual plate with the cod, sauce, then wild greens scattered around the plate, and decorate with the Bermuda buttercup flowers.

Sea Sandwort — *Honckenya peploides*

Where	Sandy and shingle beaches, South Cornwall, IOS
How abundant	Very, where found, more common on IOS
Edible parts	Leaves and stems
Season	Spring (leaves) to autumn; it can get bitter in summer when it flowers
Nutrition/ medicinal	High in vitamins C and A, therefore used across cultures

A refreshing texture when raw, and it keeps its cucumber-like flavour when cooked or pickled.

Get the ID right!
- Fleshy, succulent plant, apparently grows to 40cm, though more likely just a few cm tall, trailing plant
- Hairless, yellowish-green, with lighter coloured stems
- White flowers with five petals, flowers shorter than leaves

Suggested recipes and uses
Fresh in salads and garnishes (use instead of, or in addition to, cucumber). Cooked in fish soups or risottos, *al dente* in stir fries. Pickled, you can use it whole in salads, in salsa verde (pages 86–87), or tartar sauce.

Tips
Take care when picking, as roots are shallow and easy to dislodge. Wash thoroughly – it can be quite sandy. Keeps well in the fridge for a few days. Best in spring, can be a little bitter late summer onwards.

Sea Sandwort Salsa Verde

Ingredients (serves 4)

Pickle
- Fresh sea sandwort: stem and leaves
- White wine vinegar, to cover the plant
  (*This must be prepared **a month ahead***)

Salsa verde
- 1 garlic clove
- 4 anchovy fillets
- 60ml pickled sea sandwort
- 1 large handful flat-leaf parsley, with stalks
- Juice of half a lemon
- 1 shallot, finely chopped
- 2–4 tbsps extra virgin olive oil
- Sea salt and black pepper to taste

This is quite a punchy salsa verde (green sauce). The combination of lemon and vinegar really brings it alive. You'll need to make the pickle a month in advance. The proportions of different ingredients in a salsa verde can be varied according to tastes, so feel free to experiment with different herbs or amounts. Serve with fish, roasted meat or vegetables. Also good on toast or with pasta.

For the pickle: First wash, then place the plants in a saucepan, cover with vinegar and bring to a simmer. Take off the heat immediately, allow to cool and store in an airtight, sterilized jar, ensuring the plant is completely submerged in the vinegar. Leave for at least one month, but can be kept for up to a year.

For the salsa verde: Chop by hand, or in a food processor, the garlic, anchovies, pickled sea sandwort and parsley. Add the lemon juice, then the chopped shallot and oil, little by little, tasting as you go. When adding the olive oil, stop when you have the consistency you want – you may prefer a thick or more fluid salsa verde. Taste and adjust again with salt and pepper.

Common Sorrel – *Rumex acetosa*

Where	Fields, grassland, hedgerows, Cornwall, IOS
How abundant	Very, where found
Edible parts	Leaves and stems
Season	All year round. Best avoided in summer when the plant flowers
Nutrition/ medicinal	High in vitamin C, also contains a substantial amount of vitamin A, plus B complex, E and K. Due to its high level of oxalic acid, large amounts are not recommended, as the acid can inhibit the absorption of calcium, iron, and zinc. Can also aggravate kidney stones

Get the ID right!

- Grows up to 60cm in height
- Arrow-shaped leaves that come down into a point (always to a sharp point), either side of the stem
- Stem is channelled – (U-shaped)
- Sometimes with red markings on the leaves, or pinkish at the base of the stem
- Flowers are reddish, like small discs, in bunches on stems

Suggested recipes and uses

Raw in salads, flash cook in omelettes, traditionally in sorrel soup (pages 90–91), or in a white sauce with fish. Can make a good sorbet or ice-cream, though add ascorbic acid so the green colour remains.

Tips

Use irregularly and in conjunction with milk, yoghurt or cheese to counter the binding up of calcium (see nutritional/medicinal).

A definite favourite for many, and easy to spot everywhere, once you get your eye in.

Sorrel and Pennywort Dressing

Refreshing and versatile.

Carefully wash the sorrel and pennyworts and pat dry. Place all the ingredients in a food blender and blend. Adjust flavour with salt and pepper if required. Serve as a dressing for salad, with fish, or as a dip.

Sorrel and Alexanders Soup

Simple flavours in a creamy base.

Chop the onion and put aside. Wash and dice the potato and Alexanders, and separately the three-cornered leek, then the sorrel. Slowly heat the butter in a large saucepan. When it sizzles, add the onion, and cook until soft. Add the potato and Alexanders, stock and milk. Bring to a simmer, lower the heat, cover and cook for 25 minutes. Add the three-cornered leek and cook for a further 5 minutes. Liquidize until smooth, and return to the pan. Stir in the sorrel. Heat through, if necessary, but do not boil. Serve immediately.

Three-cornered Leek –

Allium triquetrium

Where	Hedgerows and any disturbed ground, Cornwall, IOS
How abundant	Very, where found, spreads easily
Edible parts	All
Season	Spring (leaves, stems, flowers, bulbs), winter (leaves, bulbs)
Nutrition/ medicinal	All the benefits of the garlic/onion family in helping to reduce blood cholesterol, and as a digestive aid. Can support circulation, and has beneficial antioxidants, vitamins and minerals which are useful against colds and flu

Sweet, garlicky and abundant.

Get the ID right!

- Long, succulent stems, up to 45cm tall
- Stems have three corners/sides
- Smells of garlic when bruised
- Flowers are white and bell-shaped, drooping downwards, with striking green stripe on them

Suggested recipes and uses

Add into numerous dishes, including stir fries, soups, or as a raw garnish on salads, meat or fish dishes, or add into bread. Great in pesto (page 95) and sauces.

Tips

Chop leaves and stems, as they are quite fibrous. The flower stems are the sweetest, and the flowers are great as an edible decoration. Considered an invasive weed, so many landowners will be grateful if you offer to dig it up (see page 10).

Three-cornered Leek and Nettle Pesto

Ingredients (serves 4)

- 100g nettle tops, washed
- 50g three-cornered leek (ideally with bulbs)
- 50g walnuts
- 150ml (approx) extra virgin olive oil
- Juice of half a lemon
- Sea salt and black pepper to taste
- 100g Parmesan cheese, grated

A substantial pesto, best enjoyed fresh.

Steam the nettle tops for 3 minutes. Allow to cool, and squeeze out excess liquid. Wash the three-cornered leeks thoroughly and pat dry, removing excess water. Put the walnuts and three-cornered leek in a food processor and process until finely chopped. Add the nettles and pulse until the leaves are chopped. Then trickle in the oil as the processor runs, until you have a fairly sloppy purée. Add lemon juice, salt and pepper, then the Parmesan, blending until you reach a pesto consistency. Serve as a dip with bread, on pasta, with rice, or as a topping for fish or meat dishes.

References and Further Reading

It is always advised to check plant identification with an expert, never eat a plant unless you are 100% certain you have picked the right one. Rachel Lambert leads public foraging courses and offers private tuition where you can ask questions, and check your identification queries directly with her. Courses are very hands on, with the focus on building your practical foraging skills. You can find out more on: www.wildwalks-southwest.co.uk

Bunney, Sarah, ed. (**1984**), *The Illustrated Book of Herbs: Their Medicinal and Culinary Uses*, London: Octopus. Over 250 species in full colour

Hall, Dorothy (**1972**), *The Book of Herbs*, London: Angus & Robertson

Hatfield, Gabrielle (**2007**), *Hatfield's Herbal: The Secret Society of British Plants*, London: Allen Lane

Houston, Fiona, and Milne, Xa (**2008**), *Seaweed and Eat It: A Family Foraging and Cooking Adventure*, London: Virgin Books

Irving, Miles (**2009**), *The Forager Handbook: A Guide to the Edible Plants of Britain*, London: Ebury Press

Mabey, Richard (**2012**), *Food for Free*, London: Collins

Ody, Penelope (**1993**), *The Complete Medicinal Herbal. A practical guide to the healing properties of herbs, with more than 250 remedies for common ailments*, London: Dorling Kindersley

Phillips, Roger (**2014**), *Wild Food: A Complete Guide for Foragers*, London: Macmillan

Rachel Lambert (**2017**), *Seaweed Foraging in Cornwall and the Isles of Scilly*: Alison Hodge Publishers

Surey-Gent, Sonia, and Morris, Gordon (**2000**), *Seaweed: A User's Guide*, Surrey: Whittet Books

Wong, James (**2009**), *Grow Your Own Drugs: Easy recipes for natural remedies and beauty treats*, London: Collins